THE *BEST* OF SUNNY-SIDE UP

by Doug MacGregor

Published by
Doug MacGregor
Fort Myers, FL

Library of Congress Control Number: 2001117322

ISBN: 0-9654843-1-9

The contents of this book originally appeared in The News-Press of Fort Myers, ©1997, ©1998,
©1999, ©2000, and ©2001. All cartoons are reprinted with permission of The News-Press.

Color printed in the U.S. by The News-Press Publishing Company, Fort Myers, Fla. USA

This book is dedicated to all those loyal souls who start their day reading a newspaper...

Autographed especially for: SUELLEN FOXIE

BEST ALWAYS —

DOUG MacGregor

HAPPY HOLIDAY 2001!

Never mind pea and golf ball-size hail, how about the VW-size hail ?!!

Jack couldn't get to the supermarket to buy dinner because of a heavy downpour. But, it turned out to be his lucky day as three walking catfish came in off the street.

Late for a very important appointment, Jeff luckily remembered to put an umbrella in the car. Too bad he put it in the trunk.

When Henry opened his car door, he was greeted with a tidal wave. That was the last time he'd crack his window more than an inch during the rainy season.

The backyard lawn sprinkler show wasn't quite like Waltzing Waters, but the neighbors seemed to like it, nevertheless.

Why do we see lawn sprinklers on in the middle of a huge afternoon downpour?

During the summer flash flood months standard equipment on all Florida cars should include snorkle, mask, fins, and periscope.

Everyone makes fun of monster trucks around town until flash floods hit.

Merle and Mildred braved the outdoors in the middle of the hurricane. Expecting to see the eye, they were astonished to spot the *nose* instead.

Clouds over Southwest Florida beaches.

Familiar cumulofaucet clouds during
Southwest Florida summer afternoons.

Mrs. Jones had just gone in to get a loaf of bread
when the skies opened up. Trapped for an hour
inside she would now try to find her car.

You know it's hot when the AC trucks
in town get a police escort on house calls.

When the new area ice rinks are built, people
will gladly fall on their fannies all day just to beat
the summer heat.

The Jetson family avoids the bumper-to-bumper hurricane evacuation aggravation.

Fred took advantage of the Firestone recall and provided recycled hurricane protection for his home.

Right there next to the beach parking meter you'll find the coin-operated wildlife entertainment machine.

Where there's a nude beach there's usually a popular fishing hole not far offshore.

The annual sting ray shuffle along the Gulf shores.

Jack learned his lesson the hard way –
never leave an open bag of snacks
unless you want to be kidnapped by
a hungry flock of seagulls.

Hank and Harvey forgot to bring the frisbee to the beach. That didn't stop them from taking up a game of horseshoe crab horseshoes.

Little Billy loved the water. He could stay in it for hours on end. The sting rays and jelly fish never bothered him. It was those barnacles he hated to have his mother remove.

Shiver-me-timbers! Brad and Billy found
a lot of cool things on their eroded beach, but
discovering Blackbeard's skeleton was one mom
and dad would find hard to believe.

"Get outdoors!", shouted Joe's wife. "All fall you
just lay on the couch and watch TV." So Joe
went outdoors and to his surprise the sunset that
night was hauntingly familiar.

15

Beach etiquette rule #1
Never practice your sand wedge shots when their are people in close proximity.

"How many times do I have to tell you not to go diving for fish on the sandbar!"

Two flamingos elope to Lovers Key
and tie the knot.

When your friends bury you on the beach
be sure the tide is going out before they
decide to go to the store.

Sarah found a pair of giant angel wing shells
on the beach. And as the saying goes,
"If the wings fit, wear 'em."

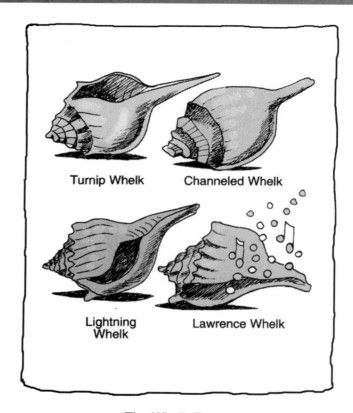

Turnip Whelk Channeled Whelk

Lightning
Whelk Lawrence Whelk

The Whelk Family.

Miracle of miracles! The latest El Nino storm washes the rarest retired Beanie Baby whelk on to the Sanibel shoreline.

In the winter you can always tell the locals from the tourists by their bathing suits.

At first Chuck and Chester thought they had found a Calusa Indian mound. On closer inspection they found it was the biggest fire ant hill in Southwest Florida.

What everyone needs in their backyard –
a fresh squeezed orange juice tap dispenser.

The local kids loved Mr. Jones.
He was the only one in the neighborhood
with a gumball limbo tree.

Roseate spoonbill varieties.

When roseate spoonbills aren't hanging out at the Ding Darling Wildlife Refuge they can be seen flipping burgers at a local fast food joint.

22

Sparky the Wonder Dog chose to stay indoors all summer. Now he finds out his master has converted his doghouse into a home for wayward sandhill cranes.

Suddenly the reception from the satellite dish got scrambled by a family of nesting osprey.

Going to the bird feeder one too many times.

When drip-drying the laundry always make room
for the neighboorhood anhinga to hang out.

Mildred gets her early morning exercise playing "Simon Says" with the plastic pink flamingos on the front yard.

Surprise! Instead of candles Susan was reminded of her age with fifty, count them, fifty pink flamingos decorating her front yard.

"Hey what are you lookin' at?! Even us snowy egrets are entitled to a bad hair day!"

"Hey Earl, I haven't spotted one blasted bird yet! How are you doing?"

If you don't like seagulls invading your beach site be sure to bring along a giant pterodactyl kite to scare them away.

Thinking you have a new hood ornamen, you will be closely escorted...by brown pelicans crossing the Sanibel Causeway.

Chisels and jackhammers won't cut it.
The only thing that will remove those rock
hard *mud daubers* is a category five hurricane
power washer.

Mailboxes around Southwest Flordia.

It wasn't the snakes, fire ants or walking catfish that shook the neighborhood after the flash floods. It was those dang loud frogs!

"Alongside your mango margarita we will be serving a mashed mango souffle, mango fricassee, with mango dumplings, and for dessert a choice of mango custard, or mango pudding."

Forgotten keys around southwest Florida.

In-line skates.

Portuguese
Man-of-War

Portuguese
Man-of-Peace

Cruising comfortably at ten knots a paradise
boat suddenly encounters *heavy chop.*

"Oh wonderful, just what I've been
been waiting for – early-bird coupons."

Captain Mac was out for a relaxing sail. Then suddenly he got caught in a gust of 30 knots!

Peter knew he could outrun the cigarette boats especially with a category five hurricane on his side.

Catch of the day.

The local tarpon tourney ends early
when everyone hooks the only prize catch at
the same time.

Ed and Frank's day-long fishing
expedition turned into a sunset cruise thanks
to a 250-pound tarpon that wouldn't quit.

How to catch flying fish.

After another three-hour tour, Gilligan, the Skipper, the Howells, the Professor, Mary Ann and Ginger end up stranded on one of the Ten Thousand Islands.

The charter captain was heard to say, "Yep, I can assure you I've got a secret fishing hole *no one* has ever seen or heard of."

Beware of the elusive and cunning sawfish.

Local fishermen don't count sheep to take a nap,
they count dolphin.

Joe's slice placed him in yet another precarious position. Luckily he had one more trick club left in the bag – his safe and trusty five iron with a 30-foot shaft extender.

When Charlie's ball landed roofside on the 12th hole, he didn't panic. Instead he played the old Happy Gilmore rain gutter shot to save par.

Never trust local golf course squirrels to steal just snacks. They'll take the whole darn cart if you let them.

Fred and Charley thought they had followed their drives carefully. However, they forgot to look in the ball-eating sabal palm tree in the middle of the fairway.

39

Jack didn't mind hitting balls out of bounds.
It gave him a chance to take home a month's
supply of balls and a few snake skins.

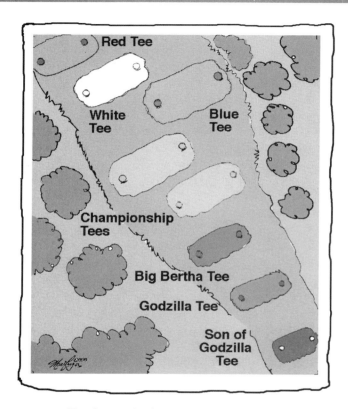

Tee boxes in the modern era of golf.

40

What the locals call a "gator gimme."

Angry Al hated the first hole. And he had enough broken clubs by the tee box tree to prove it!

All day Oscar kept telling his ball to "get legs." Finally it did.

The new titanium iron for the high rough.

If you live on a golf course it is always common courtesy to provide errant hackers with a target to improve scores.

There wasn't a cloud in the sky save for the one that kept following Fred. The more frustrated he got the harder it would rain.

After marking down an eight on every
hole Frank suddenly turned into Frosty.

Fred made two mistakes on the third hole.
First he duck-hooked his drive into the nearby
driving range. Second, he tried to find it!

44

Known for his massive drives, Big George always brought along some extra course maintenance equipment.

Joe ran out of golf balls by the ninth hole. Not worried, he knew right where to go to buy a new supply. Unfortunately, it would cost him an arm and a leg.

The ol' reliable super magnet retrieval system.

Helen doesn't need a Big Bertha because
she consistantly drives her ball down
every cart path 350 yards.

Bob got his first hole-in-one with a
little help from some regular visitors.

When throwing clubs, be careful not to bend
them like a boomerang or they will come back
and hit you when you least expect it.

The typical Collier County golf cart and
one from Lee County.

The good news was Jack found the lowest
spot on the course when the storm hit.
The bad news was he forgot to retract his
ball retriever.

Paul Bunyan golf vacationing
in Southwest Florida.

The giant blue heron wasn't scared.
Floater balls never hit their target at the
hackers' driving range.

49

Murphy starts his mower for the first
time this season.

Just how fast does the grass grow in
the summertime?

Charlie always gets out the ol' army helmet when mowing under the dead weight of royal palm fronds.

Jack's brand new super deluxe leaf blower launches him skyward.

Mr. Jones wasn't sure if it was the El Nino winter or that new fertilizer, but he now owned a treehouse thanks to the backyard banyan.

Bob took pride in the fact that he had the only perfectly straight Norfolk Island pine tree in the whole county.

The neighborhood prowler meets his match
as he backs into a strangler fig tree.

Mrs. Smith didn't need to put up
No Trespassing signs. She had a barrier of
silk-floss thorn trees surrounding her property.

Harold thought he was doing himself a favor by finishing the lawn after dark. Of course the next morning he discovered he had missed a few spots.

Washingtonian palms provide the best view for backyard treehouses.

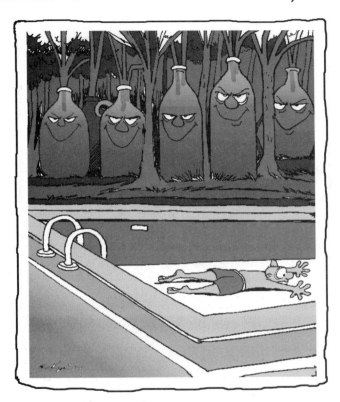

Ahhh! There's nothing like the smell of mashed potatoes when the melaleuca trees are in full bloom. It makes you want to go roast some turkey.

Charlie knew he should have cut down the thirsty melaleuca trees bordering his pool.

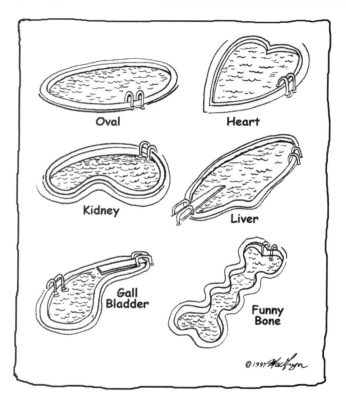

Pool shapes around southwest Florida.

Paradise in the backyard pool

As backyard pool temperatures drop
locals turn to wetsuits to take a dip.

Due to winter evaporation always check water levels when skinny dipping at night in the neighbor's pool.

One day Jim cranked the suction on the pool vac up one notch too far.

In the peak of the summer the pool
turns into a 10,000-gallon bathtub.

The seven-foot inflatable mermaid pool lounger
was Fred's favorite Christmas gift.

Palmetto bugs are so large in southwest
Florida that on some days they can be spotted
in used car lots.

Home, home on the range where the cars
and the cattle both play.

Hearing there is little culture in Southwest Florida, a local seafood restaurant places Mozart on the menu with the help of a fiddler crab chamber orchestra.

Early bird special customers.

Charlie was out for a leisurely paddle on the lake. Then suddenly it dawned on him that he had boarded the wrong kayak at the dock.

Brad has a loud snore that resembles the mating call of an alligator. During the spring he attracts the entire swamp to his front yard.

During mating season gators get customary
right of way.

"Hey honey, did the neighbors ever find their
nine-foot pet iquana that got loose last month?

Being in seclusion for months the Florida skunk ape finally enjoys a night out on the town among friends.

Elvis cooks s'mores with some uncommon friends in downtown Fort Myers.

Elvis is sighted along Summerlin Road
in Fort Myers.

Elvis is sighted in an all-you-can-eat
seafood restaurant.

On the first day of Christmas my true love gave to me – a pink plastic flamingo in a palm tree.

On the second day of Christmas my true love gave to me – two trained dolphins to taxi me on water.

On the third day of Christmas my true love gave to me – a new bead-seated chrome-plated three-wheeler.

On the fourth day of Christmas my true love gave to me – a four-gallon blender to make enough margaritas for all the visitors from up north.

On the fifth day of Christmas my true love gave to me – a five-speed swamp buggy to get through the next El Nino.

On the sixth day of Christmas my true love gave to me – a six-pack of tropical flavored liquid Viagra.

On the seventh day of Christmas, my true love gave to me – seven roseate spoonbill chefs to help prepare the holiday cookies.

On the eighth day of Christmas my true love gave to me – eight all-you-can-eat early bird coupons.

On the ninth day of Christmas, my true love gave to me – a nine-hole practice putting green for the backyard.

On the tenth day of Christmas, my true love gave to me – ten flying fish to get me around holiday traffic on U.S. 41.

On the eleventh day of Christmas, my true love gave to me – an eleven-foot kayak for two to watch Santa from Estero Bay.

On the twelfth day of Christmas, my true love gave to me – size twelve extra-wide Gator slippers to watch the Orange Bowl comfortably.

Reindeer Games of Southwest Florida
The annual golf cart polo match.

Reindeer Games of Southwest Florida
Shuffleboard matches go faster when you serve
up two disks at a time.

Reindeer Games of Southwest Florida
The annual coconut palm shot put challenge.

Reindeer Games of Southwest Florida
Night golf is no problem when Santa makes
Rudolph the cart hood ornament.

New Year's Resolution #20
I will direct the sprinkler system away from the
neighborhood sidewalks.

New Year's Resolution #34
I will go to the beach more than once this year.

New Year's Resolution #33
I will remember to turn off my right blinker
when not turning.

New Year's Resolution #57
I will be able to tell the difference between
a heron and an egret.

75

Under quiet moonlit evenings you can spot the
Cape gondolier giving romantic rides up and
down the hundred miles of canals.

There it was! Deep in the backwoods of the
Cape's Yucapan sat the Lost City of Atlantis!

Contrary to local lore, manatees have been
known to steal hot water heaters under
the cloak of winter darkness.

<u>Prehistoric Cape Coral</u>

Up to this point Ponce de Leon was flawless in his sense of direction. Of course he had yet to enter the land of Cape Coral.

Pine Island sightseeing tour vehicles.

As the rainy season ends inhabitants of
Bonita *Springs* recoil to ground level.

Bruce and Caroline had the welcome mat out since November for northern friends and family. Now at the end of April they finally get their home back!

Tommy wondered if the tent meant the circus had come to town. His dad said, "No, it hasn't." Instead, he said, "Termites have gone to town on our house."

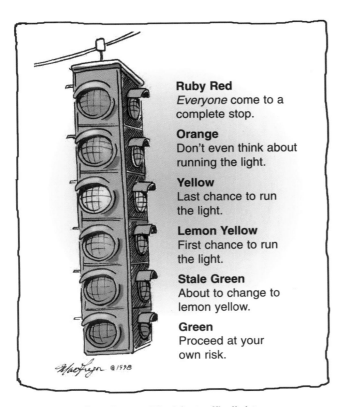

Ruby Red
Everyone come to a complete stop.

Orange
Don't even think about running the light.

Yellow
Last chance to run the light.

Lemon Yellow
First chance to run the light.

Stale Green
About to change to lemon yellow.

Green
Proceed at your own risk.

Southwest Florida traffic lights.

Hot mitts are stardard equipment in local cars during the peak of hot summer months.

Unfinished paint-by-number sunset.

New Year's Resolution #34
I will see the "green flash" at sunset
at least once this year.

What really killed off all the dinosaurs?
Well, while vacationing in Southwest Florida
they couldn't handle the heat and humidity
in the summer.

Marge's car melted after she forgot to
crack the window before she went in shopping.

The Canadian Snowbird.

The popular Ohio Snowbird.

The ever-present Michigan Snowbird.

The ever-prevalent Cheesehead Snowbird.

Boiling in the hot summer sun, the giant crab atop the Hooters roof searches for a backyard pool to cool down.

Howie had an ongoing bet with his spring breakin' buddies that the end of the rainbow would improve everyone's eyesight. Some bet.

Not to be confused with the San Adreas fault line, the 'Nole-Gator canyon splits the state in two in November.

The Sunshine State shows off its fall colors.

Red tide in morning, bathers take warning!

In May the locals finally venture to the beach
and bravely test the 83-degree waters of the
Gulf of Mexico.

Home of the purple Martins.

Could it be? Yes it is! The birders' rarest of sightings – the greater yellow-winged blue-faced black-backed long-tailed gull-billed white-bellied booby!

Purple mountain majesties in southwest Florida:
the jacaranda tree

Jenny thought she owned the brightest candy
apple red car in the neighborhood. However, it
paled in comparison to the poinciana trees down
the street in full bloom.

The Paint-By-Number Art School
of Coral Reef Fish.

Out for a night swim, Jack became
The Creature from the Green Lagoon after he
forgot to treat the pool for a solid month.

Sea-through mural art on beachfront property.

The portable igloo cabana chair is a must for
the summer beach season.

Jellyfish come in many flavors around
Southwest Florida.

Joey made good use of the starfish he
collected to celebrate Fourth of July
weekend at the beach.

Spring breakers using sunscreen
from left to right:
SPF #45, SPF #30, SPF #15 and cooking oil

Spring breakers arrive and take a course in
Dermatology 101

The rainbow all those heavy Dow Jones
investors see out on Sanibel and Captiva.

The once-in-a-millenium quadruple rainbow.
Make *four* wishes!

Doug MacGregor has been a cartoonist for The News-Press since 1988. He draws daily editorial cartoons including his popular Sunday feature "MacGregor's Boulevard" for the opinion page. His comic feature "Sunny-Side Up" appears Wednesday, Thursday and Friday in the Lifestyles section.

Doug is a native of Binghamton, NY and a 1979 graduate of Syracuse University. He began his career as editorial cartoonist for the Norwich Bulletin in eastern Connecticut in 1980.

He has won several state and national cartooning awards including Best of Gannett, Society of Professional Journalists/Sunshine State and Florida Press Club top honors.

Doug is a member of The Association of American Editorial Cartoonists and The National Cartoonist Society.

When Doug isn't at his drawing board you can spot him at local schools talking to students about cartooning, current events and the importance of reading a daily newspaper.

His cartoons can also be seen online at: www.news-press.com

Doug MacGregor